THE NATURAL HOME

THE NATURAL HOME

TRICIA FOLEY

PHOTOGRAPHS BY MICHAEL SKOTT

TEXT BY JILL KIRCHNER

CLARKSON POTTER/PUBLISHERS

NEW YORK

OTHER BOOKS BY TRICIA FOLEY

Having Tea

Linens and Lace

The Romance of British Colonial Style

To Anne Wallau,
whose natural home will always be an inspiration to me

Published by Clarkson N. Potter, Inc., 201 East 50th Street, New York, NY 10022.
Member of the Crown Publishing Group.

Random House, Inc. New York, Toronto, London, Sydney, Auckland

CLARKSON N. POTTER, POTTER, and colophon are trademarks of Clarkson N. Potter, Inc.

Manufactured in China

Library of Congress Cataloging-in-Publication Data
Foley, Tricia.
The natural home / Tricia Foley; text by Jill Kirchner; photographs by Michael Skott.
Includes index.
1. House furnishings. 2. Interior decoration. 3. Nature (Aesthetics) I. Kirchner, Jill. II. Title.
TX315.F653   1995
645—dc2   94-22263
ISBN 0-517-59668-7
10 9 8 7 6 5 4 3 2 1
First Edition

CONTENTS

ACKNOWLEDGMENTS

To Michael Skott, whose devotion to quality and natural materials has always been inspiring; to Jill Kirchner, whose way with words has captured my philosophy so well—my sincere thanks. Thanks and appreciation, too, to family and friends who shared their home and lifestyles with us for this book: Mary and Kirby in Connecticut, Thomas O'Brien in Bellport, Ellen O'Neill in Sag Harbour, Anne Wallau in Rhode Island, Paula and David Schaengold in Southampton, and Carol and Tim Bolton in Fredericksburg, Texas. And to my agents, Deborah Geltman and Gayle Benderoff, and Lauren Shakely and Howard Klein at Clarkson Potter, many thanks for their continued support and enthusiasm. And my gratitude as well to all at Clarkson Potter who helped make this book happen: Diane Frieden, Mark McCauslin, Joan Denman, and Maggie Hinders.

PREFACE

A S I SIT AT MY KITCHEN TABLE, I THINK OF THE IMPORTANT ROLE IT HAS PLAYED IN MY LIFE. I FOUND IT, BATTERED BUT STILL proud, in an old barn, and immediately decided to rescue it. A Good Samaritan came along to help as I struggled to fit it through the window of a summer rental, and later became a good friend. Fifteen years later, the old pine table, six feet long and with a few more rustic dents and scratches, is still the heart of my home in the country. It has seen romantic dinners by candlelight, Christmas cookie making with my nieces, and many book-writing sessions. I have pored over garden catalogs here with cups of tea on dreary winter mornings, repaired old linens, worked on my taxes for days on end, and had pizza parties with the twins sitting on phone books with checked homespun towels tied around their necks. . . . The stories this table could tell!

I have found that over the years I have come to rely on certain basics in my home: the big old sofa in front of the fireplace that I can never part with and just re-cover periodically, the huge white buffet plates so useful with a big family, the simple linen curtains on the windows, and the sisal rugs on the old pine floors. As the seasons change, pots of tulips are replaced with pitchers of Queen Anne's lace, then branches of bittersweet in the fall, and evergreens for Christmas. Collections and personal memorabilia change and evolve as my life changes and evolves, but it is the simple things that I find comfort and pleasure in. On the following pages you will find a few of my favorite things.

TRICIA FOLEY

INTRODUCTION

B OUGHS OF FRAGRANT LILAC IN A WATERING CAN, THE SCENT OF GRASS AFTER A RAIN, THE SMOOTH SURFACE OF A STONE WORN by the tide—these are the simple elements of nature that never fail to give us pleasure. Many of us feel a yearning for a simpler life, one more attuned with the natural world, based on pleasures rather than possessions, guided by needs rather than trends. At the same time, we are becoming more aware of the earth's limited resources, and the necessity of doing more with less. These desires dovetail in a way that allows us to live a life in greater harmony with both our selves and our surroundings.

Although it is more than just a style, this return to nature doesn't sacrifice aesthetic standards. Instead it suggests new ones: seeing the beauty in the textures and subtle shadings of natural materials, appreciating the serenity in a sparely furnished room. It suggests a way of life that is at once simple, beautiful, and environmentally sound. Like the Shakers, whose approach to design reduced every object to its purest form, the natural home distills each element—walls, floors, furniture, light—to its natural essence.

Gentle Breezes The natural home begins with the elements of nature, and letting in the fresh air is an important first step. The friendly slap of the screen door in summertime, the whirring of overhead fans—these old-fashioned sounds of ventilation are returning to our lives and helping us with energy conservation. Breezes carry the sensual fragrances of the garden into the house (even an apartment on a high floor can have a window box of scented flowers) and lift the curtains so that they shift patterns of light or warn of impending storms. Heavy window drapes, which block the smooth flow of air from room to room, are out of place in the natural home, but window shades and simple cotton curtains serve the same purpose without keeping us from enjoying the world beyond the windows.

The Light of Day It seems like common sense, but only recently have designers and builders rediscovered the importance of "daylighting"—using natural sunlight to illuminate rooms. Natural light feels better to the eye, lifts the psyche, consumes less energy, and provides better illumination. Larger windows, old-fashioned clerestory and transom windows, French doors, skylights, or even a sunroom or greenhouse all increase natural light. In darker rooms and in winter, light-colored walls and furnishings, windows that are open to the sun—not obscured by window treatments—and mirrors help bring in and reflect light.

Nature's Palette One of the simplest and most natural ways to unify a room is to create a neutral background—shades of white, cream, beige, ivory, and gray on walls and ceiling, with bare wood floors covered by cotton rugs or natural floor coverings such as sisal. Against the serenity of a neutral shell, furniture and accessories can be appreciated for their forms and textures, and a cacophony of patterns doesn't compete for attention. Simplifying a color palette to soft whites, straw and ivory, and shades inspired by nature—pale sky blue, shell pink, the gray-green of beach grass—also lets rooms blend together naturally, without concern for color "schemes" that must be changed with every new set of sheets or wallpaper. It becomes easy to mix furniture styles, or to change one piece without having to redo the whole room. In the homes featured in these pages, every object—whether inherited or purchased yesterday, whether rustic or sophisticated—works in a given room because the decorating theme is provided by the soft color in the background, not by the type of furnishings. A natural palette eliminates the possibility of making mistakes: nothing clashes or jars the senses. These are colors that are easy to live with for a long time.

Timeworn Textures Many travelers return from a trip to Europe wondering how "decay" can look so attractive. Blessed with the antiquity of civilization, Europeans worry far less than we do about stains, scratches, and dents. In an Italian courtyard, a peeling wall graced with a gnarled vine can be a focal point rather than a source of embarrassment.

When colors are kept very simple, texture is the element that adds richness. Natural fabrics—the coarse weave of canvas, the silken surface of well-worn cotton, the nubby comfort of chenille—offer a contrast of thick and thin, rough and smooth. Furnishings can also add texture—the rhythmic weaving of wicker and rattan, the gentle ripples in the grain of wood or a peeling surface of paint, the sinuous strength in iron wrought to form. And the tufted and woven patterns in straw and sisal mats, and wool and cotton rugs, add texture from raw to refined underfoot. Natural materials invite us to touch, to use all our senses to experience an environment.

A Welcoming Seat Choosing our possessions for how well they will age is essential to living a more natural life. At the heart of this back-to-basics movement are pieces that will never go out of style: a generously sized ticking-stripe sofa, a sturdy harvest table, a downy bed with a soft cotton pillowcase. These are furnishings that have stood the test of time, that weather both changes in fashion and everyday use with enduring grace. "Recycling" furniture from the past—from family antiques to simple farmhouse furnishings—not only spares another tree but also connects us to history, even just the daily history of the family who used a breadboard so often it is now softened by a hundred thousand passes of the knife. Furnishings have a way of taking over one's life, so each object you own or contemplate bringing home should have a purpose—or two—and a place.

Outdoors and In Inviting nature into your home—blurring the distinction between indoors and out—is so important that it is remarkable how often we forget to reaffirm our connection to the outside world. Not just in summer, but all year round, we benefit from living more of our lives out-of-doors, opening up our homes to the outside, and bringing more of nature's bounty inside. Often the most beautiful decorations are found right outside the door: a basketful of hearty pinecones to keep by the fireplace, a window box of herbs to flavor foods and scent the breeze, a bowl of seashells gathered on beach walks. At the same time, living more naturally means embracing a conservationist approach to everyday life that preserves what nature we have left.

As you begin to consider your own home with this book in hand, take the time to look at each element—the chair you never sit in because its synthetic fabric scratches, the decorative objects that do nothing more than gather dust—and start to edit. Take a moment, too, to appreciate which of your possessions still have meaning or a practical role in your life.

The principles of a simple style are surprisingly easy to put into practice—they just mean doing what comes naturally. They are guided by the belief that less is more, that age equals grace, and that nature unadorned is infinitely more beautiful than anything we can devise.

LINENS & LAVENDER

T HE BEDROOM IS NO LONGER JUST A PLACE FOR SLEEPING, BUT A PLACE OF REFUGE AND AN OASIS OF COMFORT WHERE WE retreat to read, sip a cup of tea, share the stories of the day. Because these are such personal spaces, they should be arranged and outfitted with particular care.

The bed, whether a pencil post, gracefully curved cherry sleigh, or patinated cast-iron headboard, is inevitably the visual focus of the bed-room, but comfort is what makes it inviting. The necessities are a head-board tall enough for reading, a frame that has no sharp edges to snag linens or limbs, and a deep mattress chosen for its balance of support and softness.

The Bed & Bath

Bed linens woven or knitted from natural fibers—all-cotton, flan-nel, or even linen sheets; down duvets with cotton covers; wool and open-weave cotton blankets—feel soft against the skin, wear well with age and repeated washings, and "breathe" to keep you cool in summer and warm in winter. Layering creates easily adjustable warmth—from a soft featherbed underneath to thermal blankets and a quilt or cov-erlet on top. A duvet makes it simple to make the bed—and it looks wonderful even when rumpled.

In the natural home, beds wear their wrinkles proudly, lined with a topography of creases. A bed dressed in the soft shades of unbleached cotton can look just as beautiful as, and feel more restful than, a bed screaming for attention in bright floral or geometric patterns. In the same way, vintage linens—pillow-cases made of homespun or old ticking, hand-sewn sheets, Marseilles spreads and hand-pieced quilts—bring a humble grace to modern bedrooms.

In both the bedroom and bath, air and light are essential. We sleep more soundly and deeply when all the senses are soothed, with fresh air and cool breezes that calm us at night and natural light that wakes us gently in the morning. Although many people have grown dependent on air-conditioning in the summer, a ceiling fan not only has a more pleasant sound, but stirs the air to cool naturally. Architectural features such as transom and clerestory windows and French doors invite in the breeze; while awnings, vines, and trees around the house create natural shade.

Window coverings need to be chosen for their ability to provide privacy and shade, as well as light. The wooden slats on old Venetian blinds and louvered shutters have a warm glow and can be adjusted to filter in just the right amounts of sun. Café curtains (the curtains on just the bottom half of the window) and athay shades (which roll up from the bottom) shield the ground floor from prying eyes while letting in light. Natural fabrics, sewn into Roman shades or Shaker tab curtains, frame a window without competing with the view. Just a simple swag of sheer scrim may be all that's needed to enhance a vista of leafy green treetops. Skylights are a particularly wonderful way to bring in light and a slice of blue sky to the bath, without exposing the bather to the neighbors.

The bath, most of all, should be a soothing sanctuary. White tile and porcelain fixtures, old-fashioned chrome spigots, and a deep bathtub—one that lets you lie back and soak in water up to your neck—create an ocean of cleanliness and calm, with no jarring distractions. With a bar of soap scented with herbal fragrances, real sea sponges, and a pile of thick terry towels within reach of the tub, a twenty minutes' soak can restore order to the world. Natural back scrubbers, made of cedar and natural bristles, resist rotting, and a loofah (actually a plant) is the best tool for vigorous scrubbing. Tile flooring can be topped with a soft, washable cotton rug or mat, and the shower can be curtained in canvas or cotton. Wicker hampers and baskets conceal laundry and necessities such as toilet paper, while glass apothecary bottles put soaps and shampoos on display.

Scent is an especially enjoyable, and relatively inexpensive, way to enhance the pleasures of the bedroom and bath. Honeysuckle vines growing outside the window to add fragrance to the breeze, a bath sachet of chamomile, a bowl of potpourri on the nightstand, or a sleep pillow of balsam needles add the sensory riches of nature to everyday experience. When roses begin to fade, the petals can be saved to scent a dresser drawer, can be tossed into the bath, or can even be made into rose water. Sachets or ribbon-tied sprigs of lavender and santolina repel unwanted visitors such as moths from the closet.

Most important, the bed and bath are places to indulge ourselves, to create a haven in which we can feel fully rested and relaxed, and find comfort and peace at the end of the day.

OLD LINEN and home-spun dress this 19th-century bed beneath the eaves in all-natural finery. The loosely gathered linen dust ruffle on the high bed creates a long cascade to the floor. A sisal rug has been bound with cotton tape for a softer edge.

AS ON THE BED above, the same neutral palette here has a more romantic interpretation, with layers of ruffled bedcovers and rows of pampering pillows. These feminine accents contrast nicely with the textures of the rustic stone walls and a wicker chest sitting in as a bedside table.

T HE CLEAN, SPARE LINES of a painted pencil-post bed are softened by a downy duvet encased in the palest peach and white shirting-stripe cover. This is the natural bedroom refined to its barest essence—a simple bed in an island of white, with bare, mellowed pine floors and a curtainless window to let in the light.

TO GIVE AN ATTIC sitting room/guest room day-to-nighttime versatility (*above*), a Jenny Lind bed is outfitted with a twin mattress upholstered and piped in ribbed cotton cord. Pillows as deep as the bed were custom-made with covers in the same cording, with a flanged border. A fine cotton cable blanket makes a soft summer throw.

WICKER TRUNKS (*above right*) provide perfect portable storage—to slip into an unused corner and to stow extra items in a summer house. The open weave lets blankets and out-of-season sweaters breathe, and adds interesting texture to the room.

I N OLDER HOMES without many closets, ingenuity prevails. An awkward, unused corner beneath a stairway has become a bedroom closet with the addition of a clothes rod and an old lace-edged curtain (*right*).

OR BEHIND-THE-DOOR storage (*above*) a shoe bag fashioned from vintage fabric becomes a charming catchall for letters, pencils, photos, and other odds and ends.

NSTEAD OF enduring the irritating buzz of an electric clock, one woman simply keeps a beautiful old pocket watch on a chair beside her bed (*opposite*), along with a pen and paper to jot down nighttime thoughts or early-morning revelations.

A CONTRAST of textures is used in a rustic Texas farmhouse, from the smooth gleam of a sleigh bed and lavish floral prints on bedsheets to the rough-hewn stone walls and more literal interpretation of the botanical theme—pressed cuttings from the garden and woods neatly displayed on the wall. Rusting wrought-iron shelves suit the stone walls, while an elegant window inset in the stone heightens the juxtaposition of surfaces. A nubby sisal rug is an ideal floor covering for this room, bridging the indoor/outdoor feeling.

A ROMANTIC VISION, evocative of *Out of Africa*, transformed this tiny, nondescript bedroom into an ethereal hideaway (*above*). A ready-made gossamer canopy of mosquito netting drapes over an 1820s mahogany sleigh bed that fits snugly between two walls. (Even in a small room, a bed can be grand.) Rumpled antique linens look just as inviting as neatly pressed ones.

I N A SUMMER HOUSE (*right*), a gently worn bureau painted robin's-egg blue is topped with a simple still life on a dresser scarf: a miniature chest of drawers, a bloom in a clear glass bottle, a silver jewelry tray, and a painted mirror.

A COLLECTION of tiny glass pharmaceutical bottles in palest blue and green (*right*) can hold delicate buds gathered from the garden or simply catch the light on a windowsill.

W ELL-USED painted pieces are grouped together (*above*) to form a dressing table of sorts—a very basic chair and table are graced with a curlicued mirror, vintage fan, and a tray with an ever-changing assortment of seashells combed from walks on the beach.

H ERE, TWO UNUSED CLOSETS and a small bath were combined to create an airy, light-filled bathroom opening onto a master bedroom. This spacious bath is filled with old-fashioned furnishings rather than the latest gadgets. An antique pine table holds necessities as well as a bountiful arrangement of hydrangeas. Pine shelves keep toiletries within reach of the bath, and a peg rack holds a collection of vintage nightdresses.

NATURAL MOTH REPELLENTS

There are many natural alternatives to the toxic chemicals in commercial mothballs. Lavender and cedar are well-known mild repellents; other herbal remedies include santolina, rosemary, southernwood, rose hips, tansy, and mugwort. You can also try strongly aromatic substances such as camphor, bay leaves, and cloves. Make up fabric sachets filled with a mixture of several herbs, then tuck them in drawers. Or make old-fashioned pomanders from oranges studded with cloves and hang them in the closet. Store linens and blankets in old cotton pillowcases instead of plastic—it protects them from wood stains while letting them breathe.

IN WHAT WAS ONCE a small closet (*above*), the toilet is neatly tucked away behind an old pine door. Narrow shelves for toiletries line the closet wall above the commode. A matching closet on the other side of the bath holds towels and linens. Wicker hampers and racks provide additional storage.

A SLAB OF STONE found on a beach becomes a soap dish with a handmade bar of seaweed soap (*right*).

A CREAMY white palette unifies natural linens and furnishings in the bath. The wicker hamper keeps stacks of unbleached cotton towels inside and on top; a Shaker peg rack holds the towels in use. White piqué cotton skirts an old sink (attached with Velcro), and muslin sewn with self-ties makes a simple shower curtain. The old lace panels at the window are a softer look than that of a shade. In lieu of a medicine chest, an old mirror hangs over the sink.

WHAT OLD BATHS lack in built-in storage is made up in charm. A clear glass shelf displays neatly folded vintage hand towels and a pitcher to fill with flowers of the season or to stand alone.

A WHITE PORCELAIN sink with restored chrome taps defines the idea of the classic bath. Although old sinks seldom have a vanity or countertop, accessories make room for the basic necessities—a shelf holds a cup, the soap dish is wedged between spigots, and the toothbrush rests in the water glass on a metal holder.

BATH SACHETS AND INFUSIONS

Baths are one of the best ways to relax or reinvigorate yourself, and herbal scents can add to the experience. Add a few drops of scented oil directly to the tub or fill a small muslin or cheesecloth bag with herbs and tie to the faucet so that the water flows through the bag as you fill the tub. Herbs with relaxing properties would be well suited for a nighttime soak before bed; invigorating scents are good for morning or predinner baths.

RELAXING:

chamomile

hops

linden (lime flowers)

lemon thyme

jasmine

pine

valerian

vanilla

STIMULATING:

lemon verbena

peppermint

sage

rosemary

thyme

lavender

eucalyptus

juniper

I N A TINY UPSTAIRS bathroom that was once dark and dreary, the owner stripped the wallpaper beneath the eaves and liked the effect so much that he left the textured surface just as it was. Gold stars paper the heavenly ceiling. A collection of mirrors, including this large round one above the tub, help to enlarge the sense of space. A simple glass shelf set flush with the tub holds bath salts and brushes; a wire rack hanging from the tub lets sponges air-dry. Towel racks line the window frame, to let damp towels dry in the breeze.

ONCE A BOUQUET of roses is past its prime, you need not throw it away; simmer the rose petals in water (strain, then repeat) to make rosewater to scent the bath, or use the dry petals wrapped in muslin to scent drawers.

S TARFISH and a humble
stoneware bowl perch on a
shelf with the guest towels (*above*).

A LACY COLLECTION
of vintage hand towels is both
functional and decorative next to a
recycled sink (*right*).

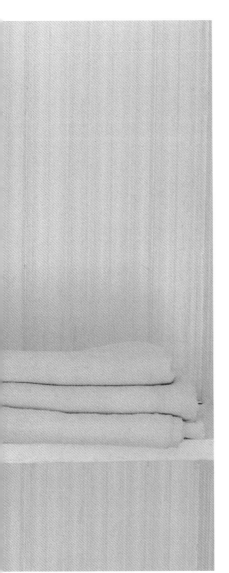

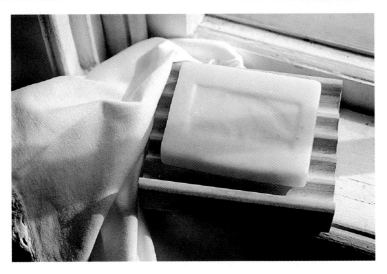

C AFÉ CURTAINS are simple to make, easy to launder, and they let in just the right amount of light (*above*). Pure soap, kept on a plain wooden holder, is one of the delights of the natural home (*left*).

A PITCHER OF WILDFLOWERS

THE KITCHEN AND DINING AREA, WHERE FOOD IS PREPARED AND MEALS ARE CELEBRATED, HAS ALWAYS BEEN THE HEART OF the home. It is where we first face the day, and where we regroup at day's end. Here is where practicality merges with our sentiments about what constitutes a home—a family gathered around the table, the bounty of the garden or shopping expeditions transformed into a feast for the senses, leisurely Sunday morn- ings spent lingering over coffee and the newspaper or watching the birds outside the window. Even at a for- mal dinner party, guests always seem to migrate to the kitchen, drawn to its nurturing warmth and conviviality.

The Kitchen

In a natural home, the kitchen may have every modern conve- nience, but its appeal is centuries old. Here the elements of water, earth, and fire mingle in objects that have the pleasingly plain lines of useful tools. Freestanding cupboards, glass-fronted cabinets, and open shelving all display functionally beautiful collections of pitchers and bowls, ceramic crocks and woven baskets. Individual pieces of furni- ture—armoires, pie safes, jelly cupboards, and sideboards—put a more personal face on storage solutions, while open shelves keep items within easy reach. Stacks of plates, nests of bowls, and rows of pitchers show off their shapely lines as well as their usefulness. Platters, trays, and copper pots hang on the wall as decoration when they are not serving at the table.

Old-fashioned, natural materials such as wood and tile counters, marble pastry slabs, and porcelain and ironstone sinks have a richness and solidity to them that is both practical and visually pleasing. Classic details such as beaded-board wainscoting and checkerboard floors frame the room, and plate racks provide open-air drying and handsome storage.

The centerpiece of the kitchen is often a large, sturdy farm table of pine, oak, or elm, worn by many washings after many family meals. Like any treasured and timeworn piece of furniture, it fills many needs—desk, dining table, work surface, counter space. Its broad expanse makes it the preferred place to do homework and crafts projects, pay the bills and catch up on work, unload the mail and groceries, and, of course, eat a meal. Because of its inviting formality, a kitchen table (or an informal dining table if the kitchen is too small to accommodate it) encourages intimacy.

The chairs that surround it need not match, but they should be comfortable and well proportioned to encourage lingering long after the meal is finished. Classic Windsor and ladderback styles, as well as chairs not generally considered "dining" chairs, such as wicker parlor chairs (often more comfortable than traditional straight-back seating), can work both around the table and around the house. They might be cushioned in a ticking stripe or faded floral print or left au naturel.

Large, unadorned windows or French doors looking out to the garden welcome natural light into the kitchen and create a connection with the world outside. A window box filled with herbs such as basil, rosemary, and dill to use in cooking or a sill lined with herb-infused vinegars and oils can also transport the scents and textures of nature into the kitchen.

Natural treasures help set the table, reflecting the change of seasons. In winter, ivy woven around a candelabra or a grapevine wreath studded with rose hips makes an inviting centerpiece. Branches of forsythia, quince, or apple blossoms brought indoors to bud or bulbs of Angelique tulips or paperwhites usher in spring. In summer, wildflowers and garden blooms and herbs look lush in almost any container—teacups, beakers, creamware pitchers, etched glass bottles, tin watering cans. A bowl of seashells evokes the moist, salt-air scent of the beach; scallop shells can serve up condiments. Even autumn vegetables—purple eggplants, flowering cabbages, a bowl of bright peppers—make bold (and edible) decoration. Cloth napkins—anything from antique damask to simple tea towels—and napkin rings add a touch of elegance and are an easy way to shift the style of the table. And because they are washable, they spare the waste of using paper. Beyond nature's bounty, candlelight, even just the simplest votives, adds something magical to the dinner table and creates a sense of occasion.

By fostering a connection with the riches of nature—simple design, simply cooked fresh foods, a harvest of flowers and branches—we rediscover the sense of well-being and centeredness that comes from feeling a part of the natural world.

I N AN OLD 1920s farm-house kitchen in Connecticut (*right and below*), shirting-stripe wallpaper adds a crisp touch to the weathered wainscoting. Found chairs and stools, all in white, some crazing with age, pitch in when everyone congregates in the kitchen. Over-sized platters hang on the wall until they are needed. Layers of linoleum were peeled up and replaced with simple gray-and-white checkerboard tile. Old kitchens may not offer the latest conveniences, but they have other benefits, like the pantry hidden behind a door in the corner.

P AINTED tag-sale dining chairs received new cham-bray seat covers (simply staple-gunned on), but kept their gently worn patches of paint. The farm table, given a sturdy coat of white deck paint, just needs scrub-downs and an occasional new coat.

S TOPPERED glass bottles in a range of interesting silhouettes can be reused to hold mineral waters or water flavored with lemon peel, sprigs of mint, a sprinkling of raspberries, or even edible flowers, like pansies. The same garnishes could also be frozen into ice cubes for a refreshing addition to lemonade, iced tea, or cocktails.

HERB VINEGARS AND OILS

Glass bottles of herb- and fruit-graced vinegars catch the sun on a windowsill and add natural flavoring to marinades and salad dressings all year long. Soak the labels off old wine bottles, then wash them or run them through the dishwasher to sterilize, and recork. At the end of the summer, harvest fruits, herbs, and edible flowers (or buy at a farmstand) to add to good-quality olive oil or white-wine vinegar. Try herbs such as basil, marjoram, rosemary, and tarragon in oils; sage, dill, or fennel in vinegars; or sweet herbs such as mint and flowers such as nasturtiums, clover, or violets in cider vinegar (for desserts or fruit salads). Blackberries look beautiful seeped into vinegar, as do golden raspberries. Or combine ingredients: Try shallots, garlic, and peppercorns in oil, or lemon balm with lemon peel.

Use one cup fresh herbs to one quart oil or vinegar. Fill a large jar or bottle with herbs, cover with oil or vinegar, and let steep for two weeks in the sun, stirring daily. If you plan to store for a while before using, filter the liquid through a coffee filter, then bottle with a few fresh sprigs of herbs. If you don't have the time for the windowsill method, you can heat the oil or vinegar to almost boiling, then pour over the herbs and let steep until cool. Strain off the herbs (they wilt) and add fresh ones as a garnish. An herb vinegar or oil in an interesting bottle makes a wonderful hostess gift—at the holidays, or to share the bounty of your garden with friends in summer and fall.

FRESH HERBS from the garden, window box, or farmer's market can be put to almost endless uses. If you can't use them right away, bundle them up and place them in the freezer, then snip off bits as needed. Or if you plan to use them within a few weeks, hang them in the kitchen for ready access. Good-quality olive oil can be flavored with fresh herbs such as rosemary, chives, or tarragon. With or without a rub of garlic, the oil makes a delicious dipping sauce for crusty, fresh-baked bread and is more savory and healthier than butter.

WITH THE ADDITION of a few shelves, unused space at the top of the stairs becomes a handy spot for a recycling center. Generous wicker baskets are attractive and efficient containers for bottles and cans; newspapers can be stacked and tied with twine. To keep the baskets clean, rinse out periodically with a hose or in the bath, and let them air-dry upside down.

S UNLIGHT is an essential feature of the natural home. It streams into this windowed alcove in a Sag Harbor, New York, summer house (*above*), where a small café table and chairs create an intimate dining corner or a spot to watch the garden's progress. The floors are bare, the windows unadorned—the better to appreciate the graceful eloquence of the metal chair and table.

F LAVORED OILS and vinegars (*right*) lined along a windowsill catch the light, showing off their ingredients—peppers and chives, herbs and flowers. Inside etched-glass and stoppered bottles, the seasonings infuse their flavor and scent into olive oil and cider vinegar, to be used for flavoring salad dressings, marinades, and sauces.

A N OLD-FASHIONED laundry center is created from a hall corner. Baskets hold linens waiting to be ironed and clothespins for fresh-air line-drying. Salvaged wooden ironing boards make a chore more aesthetically pleasing (a towel can be placed on top for padding).

OFTEN, it's the small nooks and corners—places to work in peace or nurture daydreams—that make a house special. In a tiny niche in a Rhode Island kitchen, a maple writing desk is nestled beside the fireplace and beneath a window—the owner's favorite place to start the day with a cup of coffee or catch up on correspondence. Personal treasures—a tin church, a lantern to light in the evening, a sap bucket bursting with roses, old handmade flowerpots, a lucky horseshoe—give the space comfort and meaning.

THE SHAKERS, masters of aesthetic practicality, used peg racks to hold benches and chairs (especially helpful for sweeping the floor) and to hang baskets, utensils, clothes, even clocks. Lining the perimeter of a room, pegs were always within reach, and spared the walls a pattern of nail holes. In a country home, peg racks hold string bags (a visible reminder to be taken to the market), aprons, and kitchen tools. A lower rack can be used by children for jackets, scarves, and hats, or in the bathroom for towels and robes. Ever useful, peg racks also have a pleasing simplicity and make of whatever hangs on them an interesting display.

FURNISHINGS MORE typical of a living room give this kitchen warmth and easy elegance. Comfortable wicker tub chairs pull up around a painted farm table; they can be cushioned or left bare. Instead of typical cabinets, a large pine armoire stores china, flatware, and linens in style.

A CENTER ISLAND in a spare 1800s kitchen contains nearly everything in one neat rectangle—sink, stovetop, dishwasher, work counter, cabinets. All that's left are a refrigerator and the pantry— and an open living space in which to enjoy the fireplace or the view out the windows. Wainscoting and a butcher-block top cover the island, helping the modern features blend into the room's age-old surfaces.

A NEW, NATURALLY GLAZED TEAPOT by Barbara Eigen looks right at home with Wedgwood creamware—ivy-patterned cups and covered jars from the 1920s—and simple ironstone bowls and platters.

BIRDS' NESTS ON BOOKSHELVES

PARED DOWN TO ITS ESSENCE—NEUTRAL WHITE WALLS AND NATURAL FLOORS—AND FURNISHED WITH WELL-LOVED (RATHER than "no-touch") pieces, the living room has an unexpected elegance that comes from simplicity and serenity. Instead of knickknacks, fancy fabrics, rugs that must be carefully protected, or furnishings that are uncomfortable or unusable, the natural living room has a simple style that inspires family and visitors alike to relax and enjoy.

The essential elements might *The Living Room* include a soft upholstered sofa large enough for two or three; a coffee table easygoing enough to accommodate a few pairs of feet; an enveloping chair for reading, placed near a window or a good lamp, with a small table next to it for a cup of tea. In the winter, seat- ing gravitates toward the fireplace; in summer, it opens up to the view of the outdoors. Decoration, too, is seasonal: the slipcovers change to summer whites and stripes after the first of May; heavy curtains come down, leaving only the sheers tied back to permit the breeze; and carpets make way for throw rugs or sisal. Especially in summer, when the outdoors is the focus of family life and entertaining, the furnishings should be almost maintenance free—requiring just a simple laundering or a sweep of the broom.

A love of old things can also benefit conservation, when second-hand furnishings and flea-market finds are repaired or repainted, or simply enjoyed as is. The sun-softened colors, worn texture, and gentle patina that accrue on painted and natural wood furniture over time give a richness of character that only deepens with use. Upholstered furniture can live a similarly long life slipcovered or reupholstered with fabric new or old. Simple cotton duck, white denim, or ticking-stripe slipcovers can be machine-washed for easy care. Even elegant chintzes and damasks look wonderful washed and left unironed.

Just as quilts often tell a visual family history with pieces cut from childhood dresses, so can curtains, pillows, shams, and slipcovers be fashioned from pieces of vintage fabric or embroidered hand towels and finished with antique trim. Marseilles bedspreads (with or without holes), damask tablecloths, and even fraying quilts gain a second life fashioned into cushions.

In autumn and winter, a fire in the fireplace offers glowing light and chill-chasing warmth, as well as the mesmerizing beauty of its flickering flames. With a well-designed mantel, even in spring and summer the fireplace is a natural focal point in any room it graces. To complete the natural theme, select well-seasoned wood for the longest-burning fires, save candle stubs as firestarters, and toss on a few dried pinecones for fragrance. In homes without a fireplace, a large window with a dramatic view or an intriguing piece of furniture might be a natural focus of attention.

Screens—paneled in wood or covered in fabric—are a versatile way to create different areas within a room, or hide less-than-attractive elements. And they are warmer looking, less permanent, and less intrusive than new plasterboard walls. Cased in simple muslin and crisscrossed with cotton tape, a screen can become a bulletin board, a place to tuck in mementos, cards, and pictures or to hang shells or flowers.

Wicker and woven reed baskets, trays, and suitcases are endlessly functional for organizing papers, or holding supplies on the drinks table. Baskets can gather mail, magazines, catalogs, and newspapers waiting to be recycled. Trays are particularly useful for organizing projects: letters to write, children's crafts, pencils and pens, and Christmas cards can be kept in different trays, stacked one on top of another, so everything is easy to retrieve, and easy to put away again. Trunks, hatboxes, and vintage suitcases are good stowaways for long-term storage items such as memorabilia, household records, and photographs.

Collections make a room personal, all the better if they are collections of objects with a job to do, such as baskets and pitchers. Collections from nature—berried branches, shells and stones, birds' nests and leafy wreaths—can change with the seasons. Because they are not precious, they can be returned to the outdoors without guilt when they no longer look their best. With natural things you never feel that your collection owns you instead of the other way around. Collections can also be a connection to the past—an assemblage of family photographs on a dresser, a framed assortment of old quilt squares or vintage postcards. Even a simple bowl of sea glass on the coffee table is an ever-present reminder of summers past.

I N A QUIET CORNER of an ivory-hued living room, a sofa slipcovered in khaki canvas sits next to a wicker table with a creamy tableau: a candlestick lamp, a crock of wildflowers and Queen Anne's lace, seashells, and a pair of baby shoes. A curvy white-painted chair is finished off with a delicately flounced gray-and-white-striped seat cover. Weathered wood and natural sisal are the darkest elements in this white oasis; a folding table is just wide enough for a stack of books, and the sisal rug anchors the room with its strong texture and durability.

T HE TOP PIECE of an elegantly worn and peeling mantel (*left*) was salvaged to make a wonderful shelf. Simple white Japanese tea cups rest on top.

S TORAGE IN THE
living room can be almost
any container—an old wicker hamper, a vintage suitcase or drawstring
bags made of quilting fabric (*above*).

Almost any old fabric—quilts, chenille bed-spreads, matelassé coverlets, damask napkins and tablecloths, vintage curtains, linen hand towels—can be recycled, even if torn or stained, by transforming pieces of them into pillow covers (*opposite*).

An open-air living room in Texas (*above*) is tented with canvas panels and striped Roman shades that tie back and are raised for light during the day, but come down for privacy and warmth at night. Generous ticking-stripe sofas and an old wood table are simple enough not to compete with the beautiful view.

S OFT, INVITING candlelight warms a mantel. Silver candlesticks, some in etched hurricane shades, mingle with creamware pieces, like the pitcher holding a bouquet of fresh sage.

THE GLOW OF CANDLELIGHT

Easy ideas to dress up votive candles: Wrap votives in leaves tied with raffia or gossamer mesh ribbon. Slip them into hollowed-out artichokes or lemons. Melt them into seashells. You can even float shallow candles in water. In warmer months, try placing a tray of votive candles in the fireplace for romantic light without heat. Beeswax candles are a naturalist's favorite—they're slow-burning, dripless, and naturally fragrant, and you can even roll your own from sheets of combed beeswax. Hand-dipped tapers with string wicks also make naturally beautiful candles. To make candles last longer, freeze them for several hours before using. For easy removal of candles, place a few drops of water in the holder before inserting the candle. To prevent wax dripping, use bobeches, or candle rings, to catch drips. If wax does drip on a candlestick or tablecloth, place it in the freezer, then peel off the wax. Or iron the wax off a tablecloth by placing a few paper towels over the wax and lightly passing a warm iron on top.

AN OLD PHOTOGRAPHER'S trick for getting the fire going is a good way to make use of old candle stubs (*opposite*). When you replace candles, save the stubs to use as fire starters—they are safer to use than paper, work quickly, and don't leave a residue.

THE OLD, rotted wiring from these once-electrified sconces was removed, the sconces were painted with buttermilk paint, and now they are anachronistically but romantically outfitted with candles. A small silver urn that once held cigarettes is easily converted to a vase for flowers like sweet alyssum.

A COLLECTOR'S PAS-
SION can be indulged with
an extraordinary piece like this phar-
macy cabinet. Painted in a tartan
plaid pattern, what might otherwise
be cumbersome becomes a wonderful
curiosity. The owners of The
Homestead store in Fredericksburg,
Texas, created this showcase for
their finds—and their simple gleanings
from nature create a fascinating and
beautiful display. Specially designed
iron shelves—just a double row of
prongs—exhibit a dozen different
birds' nests in all their twiggy variety. The top of the cabinet is home
to an ever-shifting array of found
objects, while the drawers catalog a
library of riches—books and cards,
seed packets and birds' eggs, leaves
and pods. There is much to look at
here, and nearly all of it was discov-
ered on hikes and walks, on forest
floors and mountainsides.

{ COLLECTIONS FROM NATURE }

- To press leaves and dried flowers, use a flower press or sandwich items between sheets of blotting paper in a heavy book until completely dry. Glue as desired onto thick paper and frame. Or use a thinned white glue to affix in a pleasing pattern on a paper lampshade.
- Arrange shells, stones, fossils, eggs, and other found treasures in a naturalist's display box. Choose a box that has a padded backing so that you can affix items with pins rather than gluing them. Or place in a glass-topped box or table for an ever-changing display.
- Glue shells or pinecones around the perimeter of a flat wooden picture frame or mirror, or on the top of a simple box. Shells and starfish look particularly at home in the aquatic environment of the bath. Hang shells from the edge of a simple window shade or the hem of a summer tablecloth to weigh it down in the breeze (you'll need shells with holes, or drill small ones).
- A straight, smooth branch can be used as a curtain rod, even in the shower. Small, sturdy branches or pieces of driftwood can serve as drawer pulls (drill small holes in the center and affix with screws).
- Dried sea urchins and starfish; acorns, nuts, pods, and moss; and bird's nests (if found on the ground) and river-smoothed stones are intriguing decorative elements on their own—sitting on a table or mantel, massed in a bowl, or lined on a windowsill. As you take nature walks, look around you with an artist's eye—to appreciate things in their environs, or to bring into your home.

S TIPPLED CREAM and brown turkey eggs (bought at a store) fill a whimsical wire basket (*opposite*)—a pretty centerpiece on a country table. Eggs from birds who have left the nest (*right*) can find a home atop a table, hung on a Christmas tree, or tucked into bookshelves. The beauty of natural collections is also found in their impermanence—when they start to disintegrate or you tire of them, they can be returned to the outdoor world where they came from.

A FRAGMENT of old wood trim forms a narrow shelf, just the right size for holding sand dollars, scallop shells, and other beachcombing finds—mementos of a sunny summer day to warm the soul in winter (*left*).

T WIGS gathered after a storm and a harvest of pine-cones serve all winter as aromatic fire starters.

Light a fire in your fireplace as a luxury, and follow these tips to use it more efficiently.

- Keep the hearth as clean as possible.

- Make small fires rather than big, roaring ones.

- Don't burn loose news-papers, which create excessive smoke. Never burn colored paper, which creates chemical byproducts.

- Don't burn processed logs regularly, because wax will build up on the flue and could start a chimney fire.

- Sprinkling salt on logs is said to reduce the amount of soot.

- Always close the flue when you aren't using the fireplace.

- Once a year, have a tradi-tional chimney sweep clean out any birds' nests or accumulated soot in your chimney before the cold weather sets in.

A CARDBOARD egg crate appropriately houses an assortment of speckled quail eggs. (Eggs should be collected only if they have fallen out of the nest and been abandoned.)

S EASHELLS collected from different beaches and from different summers are gathered on a white ironstone platter, which serves as a perfect backdrop for the natural still life. Shells also make pretty package adornments. I often give Anne Morrow Lindbergh's *Gift from the Sea* as a house gift, wrapped in plain kraft paper and tied with raffia and a seashell.

A RIPE BOUQUET of hand-picked blooms from the garden, laid across a table with a few richly colored peaches, creates a painterly still life far more beautiful than any stiff, composed arrangement from the florist. Delicate roses complement the rugged sunflowers.

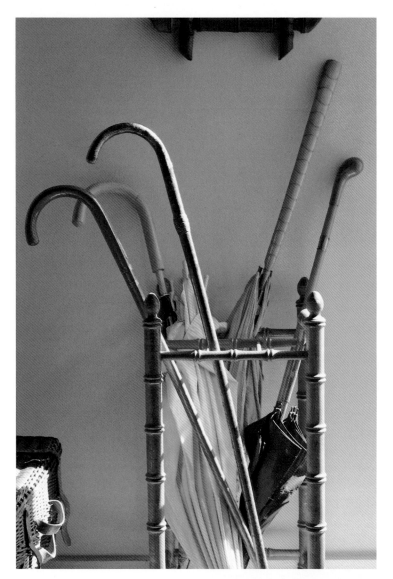

T O ENCOURAGE walks outside no matter what the weather, the English keep walking sticks and parasols at the ready in umbrella stands like this bamboo-style one—a classic country-house feature in an entryway.

F OR PROTECTION from the sun (and effortless chic), a fair-skinned gardener leaves her collection of straw hats on a table by the back door, so she and guests can help themselves as they head outside (*opposite*).

T HE WELCOMING gesture of a big bucket of wildflowers greets guests (and occupants) as they come in the door (*above*). If the entrance of a home makes a statement about the house, as it should, this one says "feel at ease." A sky-blue railing softens the stairway; when the owners ripped up the runner, they decided they liked the effect as it was.

A SHADY CORNER OF THE PORCH

A S THE WEATHER GROWS WARMER AND THE DAYS GET LONGER, WE LIVE MORE OF OUR LIVES OUTSIDE. ARCHITECTURAL AMENities such as porches, decks, and patios literally extend the house into the outdoors. Before the advent of air-conditioning, front porches, verandas, and long galleries were a common feature of many homes, especially in the South, where daily life—from dining to sleeping to just watching the world go by—was lived on the porch. Porch roofs, awnings, and deep eaves also provided shade to help keep the house cool. While northern homes might have the most windows on the south side of the house to bring in light, southern homes usually have fewer windows to block out the heat. Rocking chairs, porch swings, and gliders all recall the leisurely rhythm of life on the porch. Today, outdoor life revolves more around the back of the house than the front, and patios, terraces, and, more recently, decks have become our backyard rooms. Screened-in and enclosed porches offer a tamer, bug-free version of the outdoors.

The Outdoors

Sleeping porches, originally recommended for health reasons, now seem a purely romantic notion. A daybed can be fitted onto the porch, or, more often, a guest cottage, pool house, or converted shed provides summer sleeping quarters. Canvas tieback curtains or louvered doors allow the breeze to cool the sleeping space, but also offer protection from the rain.

Cooking and eating often move outdoors in the heat of summer, with the ease of grilling preferable to the heat of the kitchen. With a glass-topped garden table, simple picnic table, or a blanket spread on the lawn, eating al fresco becomes a special event. Lit by oil lamps, candles with hurricane shades, or, even more evocative, torches, the simplest outdoor dinner takes on a romantic and adventuresome quality.

Furniture designed for outdoor use has become so popular it is now often found indoors as well. It encompasses everything from wicker and rattan, which have been favored since Victorian times for their airy weave and portability, to ornate cast-iron garden furniture, which, on the contrary, is designed to be heavy and sturdy enough to withstand the elements. The Adirondack chair, with its comfortably sloping seat and wide, flat arms—the perfect perch for a drink—has been a summer-home classic since the 1920s. Canvas deck chairs have slipped off boats and onto land as easygoing seating. And the chaise longue seems designed solely for summer lolling. Most informal of all is the hammock: stretched between two trees or porch posts, positioned to catch the breeze, the simple cradle of netting is the gentlest way imaginable to be rocked to sleep.

From childhood on, certain elements of outdoor life become symbols of summer: running through the sprinkler, catching fireflies, crisp white sheets billowing on the clothesline, the slam of the screen door, the smell of honeysuckle. The sight and aroma of fresh-cut grass (preferably shorn by a motorless mower) recall many pleasant memories—and the clippings feed the compost heap to make a better garden.

Even in the city, small reminders of nature enrich and nurture the senses: watching statuesque branches of quince bloom inside, gathering an armful of lilacs to add fragrance to a bedroom, or growing a window box full of flowers on the sill of an apartment. Just having houseplants indoors adds a welcome touch of greenery, and even improves the quality of air.

Come fall and winter, life moves back indoors, but the ties to nature and the outdoor world need not be severed. Inside the home, sunrooms and enclosed porches, greenhouses and conservatories, even a deep bay or picture window provide a bridge to the outside, and help satisfy the craving for sunlight and greenery.

Throughout the year, bringing in elements from the outdoors helps transport the change of seasons inside. Of course, nature's bounty isn't merely decorative: pinecones and small twigs and branches can be gathered and bundled for fire starters, and dried and bundled herbs give the fire a wonderful aroma. Fresh herb bouquets are a much-appreciated favor for weekend visitors returning to the city.

Living *with* nature, rather than closing it out, is the foundation of the simple life. Nature's sensory pleasures, visual beauty, and infinite variety offer a therapeutic respite from the modern world. It's how we were meant to live.

A PICNIC in the dunes adds romance to an afternoon lunch, especially when sheltered beneath a broad, translucent Japanese umbrella and surrounded by a border of beach grasses. Even if it's just breakfast on the porch, eating outdoors seems to make almost anything taste better or more memorable. Wicker hampers and baskets pack up the picnic foods in classic, easy-carrying style. A round, open basket totes glass water bottles, and conservation-conscious real plates and flatware make the picnic as important as a dinner party.

DOWN a short, secluded verdant path, the beach awaits. The narrow, winding path, canopied in shade, creates privacy and makes what lies ahead seem even more special. Branches of beach plums can be cut and gathered on the way home for a reminder of a day at the shore (or even used to make plum jam).

P OT AMARYLLIS bulbs in November, and you'll have beautiful blossoms in time for Christmas (they take six to eight weeks to bloom). Start paperwhites at Thanksgiving—they take only two to four weeks. Look for old pots at flea markets and yard sales—filled with bulbs, they make a wonderful gift for the winter-weary.

A POTTING SHED of wooden slats on a brick foundation hides the gardener's messy labor from view and adds an attractive focal point.

SIGNS OF SPRING:
GROW A FLAT OF GRASS OR BULBS

Sometimes the happiest harbinger of spring is just a simple flat of bright green grass. Use a wooden crate or berry basket lined with plastic. Fill it with potting soil, then sprinkle the soil generously with clover or grass seed. Water and place in a sunny spot. Grass should sprout within two weeks.

Wooden flats also make rustically elegant containers for bulbs such as paperwhites, nasturtiums, and hyacinths. You can grow bulbs in crates, if you create good drainage (with holes and a saucer), or transfer flowering bulbs from bulb glasses or pots. To force bulbs, place them in bulb glasses and fill with enough water to almost touch the bulb. Change the water twice weekly. Or plant them in soil (with sand or gravel added for good drainage) so that their tips are just at soil level. Keep them in a very cool dark place, like an unheated cellar or garage, until roots and leaves about an inch tall develop (this can take three or more weeks, depending on the type of bulb). Keep the soil moist. Then create a gentle transition by moving them to a cool (ideally north-facing) window. Water the bulbs regularly, and in about two or three weeks, they will bloom—and you'll feel a terrific sense of accomplishment as you watch them evolve.

F OR TEA-TIME on a summer afternoon in a leafy corner of the backyard, a large water cooler from 1810 holds mint leaves and ice cubes for the tea. Herbal topiaries provide ready-made flavoring—try thyme, rosemary, or lavender for a different twist (freeze herbs into ice cubes for time-release seasoning). A gently faded vintage cloth camouflages a picnic table; old garden chairs sit nearby. The woven-covered bottle helps keep its contents cool.

MIDSUMMER NIGHT'S dreams take root in a tiny guest cottage/garden shed tucked into a backyard (see exterior, page 78). A banquette covered in khaki and cream ticking provides a shady spot to read or nap in the afternoon, as well as private sleeping quarters for overnight guests. Pale bead-board paneling covers the entire interior; a weathered basket makes a minimalist bedside table. A potting bench and storage for garden tools is in a small compartment off to the side. In the winter, the cottage serves as a handy place to store summer furniture.

INSTEAD OF electricity and plumbing, the guest cottage has the romance of oil lamps and candles, an elegant wind-up alarm clock, and an old-fashioned wash basin. A narrow shelf is lined with garden objets trouvés.

A TWIG NEST adorns the garden and brings the pleasure of bird song to the backyard. Feeders, birdbaths, and birdhouses, as well as berried shrubs and fruit trees, will attract a whole range of feathered friends and create a sanctuary for them in your yard.

B RILLIANT pepperberries make wonderful decoration gathered in baskets as here, or fashioned into fresh or dried wreaths, placed into a vase, hung on the door, circled around a hurricane lamp, or woven into holiday garlands.

S LEEPING outdoors—lulled by a breeze, the chirping of crickets, the fragrance of flowers—deserves a revival. In summer, the screened porch offers the best of indoors and out—light and air, but no rain or insects. This porch (screened with copper) is outfitted with a cozy daybed cased in awning-stripe canvas and striped pillows for lounging. It is also the place for intimate lantern-lit dining—the owner just pulls up a tray table and chairs. In the winter, the porch, protected with glass windows but unheated, becomes a mud room, home to galoshes and gear, firewood, and clay pots brought in from the garden so they won't freeze.

T HE SUNFLOWER-
SHAPED wire basket
(*right*) looks as if it could be a cen-
tury old, but in fact it is new—a versatile holder for bread, fruit, or
natural collections of leaves or shells.
The shells assembled atop this cup-
board are not perfect, and therein lies
their beauty—you can see the twist of
a conch shell's spine.

A N OLD pie safe (*above*)
stows garden tools, baskets,
and odds and ends; logs are stacked
underneath to dry and season.

TO MAKE FLOWERS LAST LONGER

There are tricks of the trade as well as many folk remedies and old wives' tales for keeping flowers fresher longer. Probably nothing beats clean, cool water, frequently replenished.

- Cut flowers early in the morning and immediately place into a bucket of water. Recut stems on the diagonal using a knife or garden shears, not scissors, and place into warm water.

- To revive drooping flowers, plunge stems into boiling water, let water cool, then recut the ends and put in fresh cold water. Or immerse the whole flower in cool water for fifteen minutes. If only the bloom is drooping, try pricking the stem just beneath the head with a straight pin.

- Add a little vinegar to the water for anemones, lilies, and gladioli.

- Try dipping the stems of roses, honeysuckle, and dahlias into peppermint oil.

- Dip flower stems into vodka or gin for just a few seconds.

- Drop a penny in the vase to make tulips last longer.

- Add an aspirin to reduce the growth of bacteria.

- Add a little sugar or lemonade to the water of asters, cosmos, delphiniums, peonies, and sweet peas.

- Add salt to the water of begonias, roses, snapdragons, stock, and violets.

- Place a few stalks of foxglove in an arrangement to prolong the life of the flowers around them.

- Add a few drops of bleach or a piece of charcoal to clear up murky water. Wash containers with a little bleach after using.

- Mist leaves and blossoms in hot weather.

- Refrigerate cut flowers to preserve them if you are saving them for a party or special occasion.

B OUQUETS gathered from meadows of wildflowers (*left*) scent the house with a fresh herbal aroma. Gardeners are discovering the joys of devoting some of their property to the glorious combinations of plants created by nature.

Q UEEN ANNE'S LACE (*above*) against a blue sky with clouds—a scene as stirring as any Old Master landscape. Queen Anne's lace is named for St. Anne, patron saint of lacemakers in England, and like lace, every dainty bloom has a slightly different pattern. Usually thought of as just a roadside flower, it has become one of my favorites for growing and picking.

R AMBLING ROSES branch across a weathered trellis on the side of a house in Nantucket (*above*). Trellises add an architectural element to the garden, whether in the classic fan shape or in a grid covering part or all of a wall. Arched trellises can frame a garden path or create a sheltered entry within shrubbery. They might incorporate a bench, or delineate "rooms" or sections of the garden. A pergola—a trellis-roofed walkway or patio—is even more romantic, providing a canopy of shade and scent from grape vines or climbing roses overhead. In wood or occasionally metal, left to wear softly over time, trellises lend structure to the landscape and give the garden vertical as well as horizontal form.

A S SWEET PEA vines work their way up a trellis, they create a garden "sculpture" that changes day by day (*above*). On a sunny day, laundered white cottons are hung to dry on hangers in a mulberry tree (*left*). Not only do shirts and nightgowns return to the closet naturally bleached and smelling of sunshine, they are a pleasing old-fashioned sight in the backyard.

A DIMINUTIVE guest-house and garden shed not only offers extra sleeping and storage space, but creates a focal point in a bland backyard expanse of grass. French doors open up the front of the house, and canvas panels inside can be tied back or let down to offer shade on sunny days and cozy privacy at night.

AFTER THE COOL of the sprinkler or a swim in the ocean, it almost feels just as good to be bundled up in a big, fluffy towel to dry off and warm up—even if only to get wet all over again.

F RONT PORCHES are a welcoming face on a home— and a place to live life in the slow lane. Here gingerbread detailing frames a gallery just wide enough for a rocking chair from which to watch the world go by. A bark bird feeder hangs from the eaves, and vines spill over the railing.

A FTER the delicate roses and pretty perennials of summer have faded, it's time for the rustic sunflower's moment of glory. Natural bird feeders (you can eat the seeds as well), the sunflower has a brilliant golden color and a generous size, making them a countryside favorite. They come in many varieties—from rudbeckia to black-eyed Susans—to brighten a backyard.

The Natural Linen Closet

Duvets, or down comforters, can replace a blanket and bedspread and keep you even warmer. Down is a natural insulator that's lightweight enough to be comfortable on cool summer evenings but still toasty on frigid winter nights.

Egyptian cotton is a luxurious, extra-long-staple cotton, produced mainly in northern Africa.

Fill power describes how much volume an ounce of down takes up. It's a better measure of warmth than the weight of the comforter. A 650 rating is considered high fill power.

Fox Fibre (used in Fieldcrest's New World sheets) is a cotton plant bred (by a woman named Sally Fox) to grow in different shades of brown and green, to add color naturally to fabric. (Fox Fibre is eighty percent organically grown.)

Goose down is perferable to duck down because geese create larger down clusters. Duck down generally measures 500 fill power; higher-quality white goose down starts at about 550. There is no difference between gray and white down except color. For those who are allergic to down, there are also cotton- and silk-filled comforters.

Linen is an even more luxurious all-natural fiber. Though linen sheets are quite expensive, they wear well, gradually softening with age, and last twenty years or more.

Natural cotton sheets (unlike regular cotton sheets) are not dyed or bleached and haven't been treated with chemical softeners or permanent-press or easy-care finishes.

Organic cotton comes from cotton plants grown and processed without the use of chemical pesticides and fertilizers.

Percale is a closely woven fabric with a fine finish. Percale sheets have a thread count of 180 and above, making them durable yet smooth.

Pima cotton (named after Pima County, Arizona, where it was developed) is a strong, long staple. This guarantees fewer nubs and pills.

The *staple,* or fiber, also determines the fabric quality: the longer and finer the staple, the better the quality of cotton.

Thread count equals the number of threads per square inch. The higher the thread count, the better the quality of the sheet. A count of 200 is considered high quality; the highest made in the United States is 310.

Upland cotton, with a short, coarse staple, is the most common kind of cotton grown. It is used for sheets with thread counts of 180 and less.

If you're shopping for vintage sheets or quilts, or making your own duvet cover, here are standard modern bed sizes:

	MATTRESS	FLAT SHEET	COMFORTER
Twin	39" x 75"	66" x 96"	68" x 86"
Full	54" x 75"	81" x 96"	76" x 86"
Queen	60" x 80"	90" x 102"	86" x 86"
King	76" x 80"	108" x 102"	100" x 90"

Fitted sheets should be 1 inch deeper than the mattress (usually 6 to 8 inches deep); pillowcases should be 4 inches longer than the pillow. Duvet covers should be the same size as the comforter.

STORING LINENS

Vintage and good-quality linens should not be stored unprotected for any length of time in wooden chests or drawers; the resins can stain the cloth. Protect linens by wrapping them in acid-free paper or unbleached muslin, or even easier, store them in old cotton pillowcases. Don't store them for very long periods of time with sachets, either, because the oils can eat away at the fabrics.

LAUNDERING
THE NATURAL WAY

Wash linens in natural soap flakes or at least an environment-friendly phosphate-free biodegradable detergent and warm water; do not use chlorine bleach or fabric softener. Softeners were invented to reduce the static cling of synthetic fabrics; they're unnecessary on natural fabrics. If you must use bleach, choose a powdered nonchlorine bleach such as borax. Add a teaspoon of white vinegar or baking soda to the wash to remove odors.

If linens are stained, stretch the fabric across a bucket and pour boiling water through it. If stains are stubborn and the fabric is sturdy, boil it in a stockpot filled with water and the juice of half a lemon. Let soak until water turns cold. Or presoak in borax and cold water; for old stains, rub on a paste of borax and water. Rub glycerine soap on spots such as grass, coffee, and oil to help loosen them. In the old days, linens were laid out on the lawn to dry, which is still a good all-natural way to whiten them. Or hang them on the line—you'll save energy by not using your dryer, and give your linens a fresh-air scent.

The Natural Pantry

NATURAL CLEANSERS
AND HOMEMADE REMEDIES

To make your own simple, nontoxic cleaners, all you need are basic ingredients that probably already line your pantry shelves: white vinegar, baking soda, salt, mayonnaise, flour, borax. If you prefer to buy a ready-made cleanser, choose one like Citra-Solv, Ecover, or Bon-Ami that's nonchlorinated and ecologically safe. Use cloth rags rather than paper towels.

- For a general, all-purpose cleaner, mix a cup of vinegar in a bucket of water or fill a spray bottle with one part vinegar to four parts water. Use the same mixture for washing windows with newspaper (a good way to reuse the paper) or a chamois cloth. When washing dishes, a little vinegar in the rinse water will leave crystal and glassware spotless.

- For a disinfectant cleaner for bathrooms and kitchens, mix a half cup of borax or baking soda in a bucket of hot water and apply with a sponge.

- Oven cleaners and drain cleaners are among the most toxic cleansers. For an eco-safe oven cleaner, scour with a paste of baking soda or borax. To clean up spills, sprinkle with salt, let cool, then scrape and clean. To clear out drains, pour in a half cup of baking soda, a half cup of vinegar, and a pinch of salt. Rinse with boiling water.

- To deodorize carpets, sprinkle a layer of baking soda on the carpet, leave it for an hour, and then vacuum.

- To shine silver, try toothpaste. Or put a piece of aluminum foil in a pan, layer the silverware on top, cover the silverware with water, and add a teaspoon of salt and a teaspoon of baking soda. Heat on the stove until the tarnish loosens, then let cool and wipe clean.

- To clean brass and copper, rub with a lemon sliced in half and dipped in salt, then rub clean. Or try a paste made from flour and salt with a bit of vinegar.

- Use a beeswax furniture polish or make one from vegetable oil with a few drops of lemon juice.

- To remove rings or water spots on furniture, rub in a mixture of mayonnaise and white toothpaste, then wipe dry.

- To get rid of yellow stains on china, rub with a paste of baking soda or a combination of lemon juice and salt.

- To clean old, "clouded" glass, fill with a mixture of lemon juice and crushed eggshells for forty-eight hours. Or rub stains with a raw potato and rinse with cool water.

EVERY LITTLE BIT
MAKES A DIFFERENCE

Old-fashioned thrift makes ecological sense: save soap scraps to make liquid soap, sew up in a washcloth, or to run your fingernails over before you garden, making clean-up a cinch. Instead of using pre-soaped scouring pads you quickly dispose of, try knitting up a string washcloth or using bristle scrub brushes for scouring instead. Use leftover cooking water from corn or pasta to water the plants in summer. Before there was plastic wrap, our grandmothers stored leftovers in the refrigerator

in a bowl with a plate stacked on top. Even now, using containers that can be washed and re-used is preferable to using disposable plastic products and aluminum foil.

EASY RECYCLING

- Keep canvas and string bags (as well as paper and plastic bags to be reused) on hooks near the door so it's easier to remember to take them with you on shopping excursions.

- Reduce consumption by buying less packaging in the first place.

- Buy fresh foods rather than prepackaged ones.

- Buy staples in bulk.

- Choose recyclable glass, aluminum, and cardboard containers over plastic and polystyrene that aren't as easily recycled.

- Reuse glass jars and metal cans, as people used to, to hold everything from iced tea to hardware.

- Instead of filling cabinets and pantry shelves with energy-hogging appliances, devote space to bulk storage and a recycling area.

- Bins for glass, aluminum, and paper awaiting recycling needn't look unsightly; try using large wicker baskets. Just wash them out periodically with a hose and let them air-dry.

Natural Materials and Design

A GLOSSARY OF
NATURAL FIBERS

Abaca is a shiny, thick fiber from the banana plant.

Coir is a coarse, golden brown fiber made from the coconut palm. It is less expensive than sisal, and more durable, but has a rougher texture.

Rush, seagrass, and *straw* mats are softer underfoot but not as strong as sisal or coir. They are woven into different patterns (usually in squares sewn together) and are inexpensive.

Maize is similar, though finer in texture and lightest in color.

Raffia, a Philippine grass, can be woven into mats or used to tie up packages or leggy plants.

Sisal is a strong, long-leaf fiber from the Mexican agave plant. Sisal is popular for its tailored texture (it's usually woven into tight rows), but it feels a bit rough on bare feet. It's also available in most color choices. Consider individualizing sisal mats with colored linen or jute bindings, or a border of tapestry fabric, or painting them with stencils or a wash of color.

Look for natural latex or jute backings on sisal and coir matting to add durability and reduce maintenance. To clean matting, vacuum or lift and beat clean. If the matting is not backed, clean underneath it periodically. Scrub any stains with soapless detergent. Straw mats deteriorate if they become too dry, so mist occasionally with a plant sprayer. Many wool carpets are now designed to imitate the look of sisal, and they feel much softer.

NATURAL PAINTS AND FINISHES

There are now paints, stains, and varnishes that are free of toxic chemicals, preservatives, and fungicides, from such companies as Livos and Eco Design. Water-based paints are preferable to oil-based; and old-fashioned milk paint, used in Colonial times, is being rediscovered as a naturally pigmented covering. Its muted colors and flat finish are particularly well suited to antique or country-style furniture and to stenciling floors. Buff with beeswax for a translucent finish. You can add pigments yourself to organic paint made from plant oils and resins. If you do use oil-based paints, pure turpentine or citrus-based thinner is

safer than petroleum-based synthetics for cleanup.

- If you must strip paint from wood, using a heat gun (unless you suspect it is old, lead-based paint) is preferable to highly toxic chemical strippers.

- Always work in a very well ventilated area (or ideally, outdoors) and wear a mask.

To finish new, restored, or stained wood, instead of polyurethane, choose older sealants: shellac or natural-resin varnishes, boiled linseed oil (a deep-penetrating oil that makes wood water-resistant), or beeswax, which leaves a soft luster and has a wonderful scent. Natural stains and varnishes don't have synthetic agents to speed drying, so apply thin coats and let them dry overnight or for as long as indicated between coats.

FENG SHUI: THE CHINESE ART OF PLACEMENT

Feng Shui, which translates as "wind" and "water," is the ancient Chinese art of placement. According to Chinese belief, the location of a home, the way it is sited, how the rooms are arranged, and the placement of furniture within rooms can all affect the flow of "ch'i" or energy, and bring good or bad luck to the people who live there. Many of the principles of feng shui reflect an emphasis on living in harmony with nature and one's surroundings, in a light, airy, open home. Here are some principles for arranging your own living space:

- Mirrors reflect light and give the illusion of space. They are often the best solution to open up or balance awkward corners, halls, and poorly placed doors and windows.

- Light and lamps represent the sun and are important for energy and smooth flow of ch'i.

- Plants and flowers, which represent nature and growth, can balance an awkwardly shaped space and bring nourishing energy into a home.

- Windows should open as wide as possible; ideally, opening out like casement windows, rather than only halfway up like double-hung windows.

- Stairs should be broad and well-lit; dark, narrow stairs funnel wealth out the door.

- Ceilings should be high; low ceilings can lower energy. Mirrors create a more expansive feeling.

- Exposed beams and projecting corners inhibit the flow of ch'i. Grow vines or hang mirrors to soften their edges.

- The room nearest the main entrance has the greatest importance in the home. The living room,

study, or foyer is the best room in that location. If the kitchen is the first room, the house will be food-oriented and people are likely to eat too much. If it is a bathroom, wealth will be flushed away and people will spend too much time on appearance.

- The closer the bedroom is to the front door, the less rested people will feel. The bedroom should ideally be catercorner to the front door, with the bed catercorner to the bedroom door, with a clear view of anyone entering. (Similarly, the stove should be placed in the kitchen with a view to the entrance—or use a mirror to reflect it; in an office, the desk should face the door.)

- In the living room, seating should also face the door, but not be directly aligned with it. Ideally, guests should sit facing the door, with the hosts to the side, in view of the door. Turning your back to a door literally means things will happen behind your back and can bring bad luck.

The Natural Garden

GARDEN TRICKS

- To get rid of weeds between bricks or paving stones, pour boiling water on them, or vinegar and salt. Or plant creeping thyme for a pretty border between flagstones instead.

- Physically remove intruders: Weed instead of using chemical weed killers. Pick off caterpillars and other pests from plants as you find them. Discard plants that are infected with disease.

- If you must use an insecticide, try a specifically targeted and less harmful one like Bt (bacillus thuringiensis), degradable fatty-acid soap, or diatomaceous earth. There are also botanical pesticides that are still poisonous but break down much faster than synthetic insecticides.

- Instead of using chemical fertilizers, enrich your soil with organic matter—either a commercial blend, or your own mix of organic meals, compost, or manure. Consult an organic gardening guide or your local cooperative extension to determine exactly what kind of nutrients your particular type of soil needs.

- At planting time and as protective cover in winter, mulch with compost, grass clippings, shredded leaves, pine needles, or straw.

HOUSEPLANTS THAT
MAKE YOUR HOME HEALTHIER

Research shows that plants can help filter pollutants from the air in your home. As a rule of thumb, use two or three plants for each hundred square feet. The best plants to clear the air:

Boston fern	Weeping fig
English ivy	Chrysanthemum
Tulip	Gerbera daisy
Peace lily	King of hearts
Lady Jane	

NATURAL INSECT
REPELLENTS

Certain plants are said to ward off insect intruders in the garden, and also around the house (plant outside near entrances, grow in pots indoors, place plants on the picnic table). Companion planting—growing basil next to tomatoes to control hornworms, for example—is said to help protect vegetable crops. Many remedies are folklore, but worth a try.

Ants—tansy, pennyroyal, peppermint. (Try using a mulch of tansy.)

Aphids—French marigolds, nasturtiums, pop-

pies, spearmint, chives, garlic, parsley, basil, horseradish

Beetles—French marigolds, mint, catnip

Black flies—basil, lavender

Fleas—lavender, mint, fennel, tansy

Flies—basil, chamomile, rue, tansy

Fruit flies—basil

Gnats—pennyroyal

Mosquitoes—chamomile, sassafras, pennyroyal, rosemary, sage, santolina, lavender, mint

Slugs—garlic, chives, wormwood

Weevils—garlic

Chop and scatter sweet basil leaves to repel aphids, mosquitoes, and mites. Add ¼ cup dried basil to water for a nontoxic plant spray.

Don't forget that many insects are beneficial to the garden: You can attract lacewings, which eat aphids, by planting carrots, wild lettuce, or oleander. Ladybugs, which attack numerous pests, are usually drawn to plantings of angelica, goldenrod, morning glory, and yarrow.

DIRECTORY

Earth General
72 Seventh Avenue
Brooklyn, NY 11217
718-398-4648
An eco-conscious general store
with everything from natural
linens to compost bins to home
testing kits, plus a bridal
registry.

Earthsake
1805 Fourth Street
Berkeley, CA 94710
510-848-0484
Over 2,000 items, from organic
cotton to cleaning products.

Environmental Building
Supplies
1314 Northwest Northrup
Portland, Oregon 97209
503-222-3881
Recycled and renewable lum-
ber, flooring and carpeting,
and more.

Environmental Construction
Outfitters
44 Crosby Street
New York, NY 10012
212-334-9659
800-238-5008
Ecological and allergen-free
alternatives for nearly every
building product, from paints
and adhesives to recycled glass
tiles. They ship nationwide.

Terra Verde Trading Co.
120 Wooster Street
New York, NY 10012
212-925-4533
A pioneer of all-natural products for the home, from cleaning
supplies to paints and finishes to
cotton-canvas shower curtains.

ABC Carpet & Home
888 Broadway
New York, NY 10003
212-473-3000

Sisal, coir, and other natural-
fiber carpets; all-cotton
bed linens.

And Co.
108 Washington Street
Norwalk, CT 06854
203-831-8855
Beautiful bed linens and
bath products.

Ad Hoc Softwares
410 West Broadway
New York, NY 10012
212-925-2652
European bed linens, table
linens, lotions, and basics.

The Allergy Relief Shop
3371 Whittle Springs Road
Knoxville, TN 37917
800-626-2810
Custom-made mattresses and
bedding made of organic cotton
(catalog available).

Portico Bed and Bath
135 Spring Street
New York, NY 10012
212-541-7722
Sophisticated natural bed
linens, bath soaps, and lotions.

FURNITURE

English Country Antiques
Snake Hollow Road
P.O. Box 1995
Bridgehampton, NY 11932
516-537-0606
Functional, casual country
antiques.

Homestead
223 E. Main Street
Fredericksburg, TX 78624
210-997-5551
High-styled furniture,
antiques, and accessories for the
home: Adirondack cottage style
and all-white and natural
furnishings.

Hope & Wilder
454 Broome Street
New York, NY 10013
212-566-9010
Recycled furniture and painted
furnishings from the
1920's–30's.

IKEA
1100 Broadway Mall
Hicksville, NY 11801
516-681-4532
Inexpensive Swedish basics for
the home.

Ruby Beets
Poxabogue Road and Route 27
P.O. Box 596
Wainscott, NY 11932
516-537-2802
Painted and recycled vintage
furniture and accessories.

Zona
97 Greene Street
New York, NY 10012
212-925-6750
Southwestern natural
furnishings.

HOME ACCESSORIES

Bell'Occhio
8 Brady Street
San Francisco, CA 94103
415-864-4048
Very specialized shop
with vintage accessories and
beautiful ribbons.

The Bellport General Store
125 Main Street
Bellport, NY 11713
516-286-3015
All-white and natural furnishings, new and vintage linens and
fabrics, natural soaps and
cleansers, and accessories.

Museum of Modern Art
Design Store
11 West 53rd Street
New York, NY 10019
800-447-6662
Classics of clean, modern design
(catalog available).

Takashimaya
693 Fifth Avenue
New York, NY 10022
212-350-0100
Sophisticated Japanese store
with a garden shop, antiques,
accessories for the home,
and tea room.

Whispering Pines
516 Main Street
Piermont, NY 10968
914-359-6302
A rustic shop featuring
Adirondack-style benches, candles, and accessories (catalog
available).

Wolfman·Gold & Good
Company
116 Greene Street
New York, NY 10012
212-431-1888
Classic white tabletop
collection.

GARDEN ACCESSORIES

The Gardener
1805 Fourth Street
Berkeley, CA 94710
510-548-4545
Garden center with a Zen
point of view.

Gardener's Supply
128 Intervale Road
Burlington, VT 05401
802-660-3505
Eco-friendly products for the
garden (catalog available).

Lexington Gardens
1011 Lexington Avenue
New York, NY 10021
212-861-4390
New and old garden planters,
benches, etc.

Pure Mädderlake
478 Broadway
New York, NY 10013
Eclectic assortment of containers, accessories, and state-of-the-
art flower arrangements.

Treillage Ltd.
418 East 75th Street
New York, NY 10021
212-535-2288
Elegant vintage garden accessories and plants.

ENGLAND

Chelsea Gardener
125 Sydney Street
London SW3
071-352-5656
Garden center with books,
plants, and pots.

Clifton Little Venice
3 Warwick Place
London W9
071-789-7894
Antique garden accessories,
books, seeds, with a complete
garden center.

The Conran Shop
Michelin House
81 Fulham Road
London SW3
071-585-7401
Simply styled furniture, fabrics, garden shop, creative
designs for children.

Divertimenti
139-141 Pulham Road
London SW3
071-581-8065
Kitchen shop with copper pots,
casseroles, and cooking utensils.

Egg
36 Kinnerton Street
London (Belgravia) W1
071-235-3315
Eclectic, personal collection of
robes, wood bowls, textiles with
a strong Indian influence.

Habitat
The Heal's Building (and
other branches)
196 Tottenham Court Road
London W1
071-255-2545
The latest in furniture, lighting,
outdoor furnishings, and linens.

Ian Mankin
109 Regents Park Road
Primrose Hill
London NW
071-722-0997
and
271 Wandsworth Bridge Road
London SW6
071-371-0825
All-natural fabrics for the
home—including ticking, home-
spun, checks, and canvas.

David Mellor
4 Sloane Square
London
071-730-4259
Design classics, from flatware
to the best picnic hampers.

Muji
26 Great Marlborough Street
(and branches)
London W1
071-494-1197
Japanese designs for the home—
china, storage units, linens—all
in a neutral palette.

The Shaker Shop
25 Harcourt Street
London W1
071-724-7672
Textiles, cupboards, chairs,
and classic wood peg racks.

FRANCE

Forestier
55 Bis Quai de Valmy
Paris 75010
42-45-4236
Garden accessories and storage.

Jardins Imaginaires
5 Rue D'Assas
Paris 75006
42-22-8802
Vintage garden pots and glass
bell jars.

Catherine Memmi
32-34 Rue St. Sulpice
Paris 75006
44-07-2228
Soothing shop with every
thing for the home in a soft
color palette.

Natural Company
Les Tissages D'Athis
1 Rue Diderot
Parc D'Activites des Radars
Grigny 91350
69-25-8707
Wholesale company specializ-
ing in tin and terra-cotta
containers.

Papier Plus
9 Rue de Pont Louis
Phillippe
Paris 75004
42-77-7049
Natural stationery, papers, and
handmade books and portfolios.

Rosemary Schulz
30 Rue Boissy D'Anglas
Paris 75008
40-17-0661

Terra Nostra
13 Rue Massenet
Nice 06000
93-87-9963
Natural home store.

MAIL-ORDER CATALOGS

Basketville
Main Street
P.O. Box 710
Putney, VT 05346
800-258-4553
Classic New England pie,
picnic, and log baskets.

Chambers
100 North Point
San Francisco, CA 94133
800-334-9790
The best of the bed and
bath lines—from oatmeal soap
to silk duvets.

Crate & Barrel
311 Gilmen Rd.
Wheeling, IL 60090
800-323-5461
Classic designs: canvas and
wood furniture, great glassware
and china.

Eco Design
1365 Rufina Circle
Santa Fe, NM 87501
800-621-2591
The largest selection in the
U.S. of non-toxic wood stains,
paints, and finishes (store also).

Fredericksburg Herb Farm
P.O. Drawer 927
Fredericksburg, TX
78624-0927
800-259-4372
Wonderful mail-order newslet-
ter and catalog with herbal vinegars, oils, and bath products.

Gardener's Eden
Mail Order Dept.
P.O. Box 7037
San Francisco, CA 94120-
7307
800-822-9600
Garden tools, pots, furniture,
accessories.

Garnet Hill
262 Main Street
Franconia, NH 03580
800-622-6216
All-natural-fiber bed linens,
pillows, and comforters.

Hendricksen Natürlich
P.O. Box 1677
Sebastapol, CA 95473
707-829-3959
Imported natural linoleum,
pesticide-free sisal and seagrass
with natural latex backing.

Hold Everything
Mail Order Dept.
P.O. Box 7807
San Francisco, CA
94120-7807
800-421-2264
The ultimate guide to storage,
including a variety of wicker
baskets and trays.

Maine Made
Office of Economic
Development
State House Station #59
Augusta, Maine 04333
800-872-3838 (in Maine)
800-541-5872 (outside Maine)
Pottery, baskets, woven
throws, all by Maine
craftsmen.

Natural World Inc.
652 Glenbrook Road
Stamford, CT 06906
800-728-3388
Natural cleaning supplies,
bath, and beauty products.

Nature Company
P.O. Box 188
Lawrence, KY 41022
800-227-1114
Unusual gift ideas, all with an
emphasis on saving the earth.

Pottery Barn
Mail Order Dept.
P.O. Box 7044
San Francisco, CA 94120
800-922-5507
Simple, contemporary designs
for the home—great rugs and
slipcovers.

Seventh Generation
Colchester, VT 05446-1672
800-456-1177
A terrific source for everything
environmentally correct, from
compact fluorescent bulbs to
natural cleansers to recycled
paper products.

Shepherd's Seeds
6116 Highway 9
Felton, CA 95018
408-335-6921
Classic and unusual herb
garden seeds, cutting garden
packets.

Smith & Hawken
25 Corte Madera
Mill Valley, CA 94941
415-383-2000
The best in garden design
for tools, furniture, pots, and
accessories.

The Vermont Country Store
P.O. Box 3000
Manchester Center, VT
05255
802-362-2400
Linen toweling by the yard,
old-fashioned kitchen gadgets.

Williams-Sonoma
P.O. Box 7456
San Francisco, CA
94120-7456
800-541-1262
Basics for the cook—from pots
and pans to the best brand of
vanilla extract.

FURTHER READING

Aria, Barbara. *Outside Inside: Decorating in the Natural Style.* New York: Thames and Hudson, 1992.

Dadd, Debra Lynn. *The Nontoxic Home & Office.* Los Angeles: Jeremy P. Tarcher, 1992.

Harris, Marjorie. *Better House and Planet.* Toronto: Key Porter Books, 1991.

Lindbergh, Anne Morrow. *Gift from the Sea.* New York: Pantheon Books, 1955.

Marinelli, Janet. *The Naturally Elegant Home.* Boston: Little, Brown, 1992.

Newdick, Jane. *Sloe Gin and Beeswax.* London: Charles Letts & Co., 1993.

Ohrbach, Barbara Milo. *Simply Flowers.* New York: Clarkson Potter/Publishers, 1993.

Pearson, David. *The Natural House Book.* New York: Fireside, 1989.

Rossbach, Sarah. *Interior Design with Feng Shui.* New York: Penguin/Arkana, 1987.

Tolley, Emelie, and Chris Mead. *Gifts from the Herb Garden.* New York: Clarkson Potter/Publishers, 1991.

INDEX